DREAMING AND DREAMS

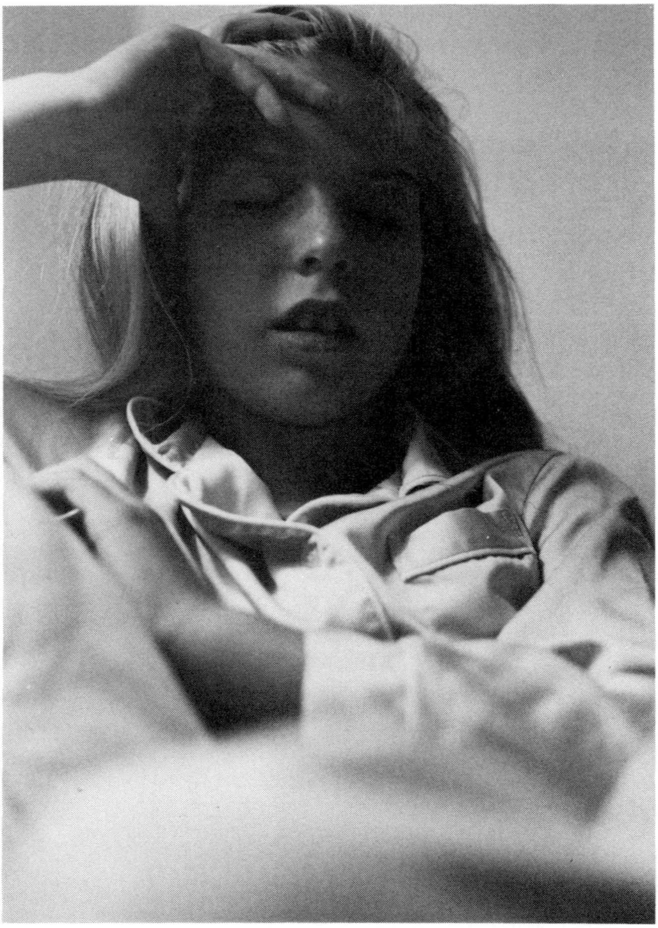

DREAMING AND DREAMS

PATRICIA STAFFORD

ILLUSTRATED WITH PHOTOGRAPHS
AND WITH DIAGRAMS
BY THE AUTHOR

ATHENEUM ~ 1992
New York

MAXWELL MACMILLAN CANADA
Toronto

MAXWELL MACMILLAN INTERNATIONAL
New York   Oxford   Singapore   Sydney

NEWTON FALLS PUBLIC LIBRARY
204 SOUTH CANAL STREET
NEWTON FALLS, OH   44444

YA
154.63
S

Copyright © by Patricia Stafford

All rights reserved. No part of this book may be reproduced or transmitted in any form or by any means, electronic or mechanical, including photocopying, recording, or by any information storage and retrieval system, without permission in writing from the Publisher.

ATHENEUM
Macmillan Publishing Company
866 Third Avenue
New York, NY 10022

MAXWELL MACMILLAN CANADA, INC.
1200 Eglinton Avenue East
Suite 200
Don Mills, Ontario M3C 3N1

MACMILLAN PUBLISHING COMPANY
is part of the Maxwell Communication Group of Companies.

First edition

Printed in the United States of America

10 9 8 7 6 5 4 3 2 1

The text of this book is set in Berkeley Book.

Book design by Black Angus Design Group

LIBRARY OF CONGRESS CATALOGING-IN-PUBLICATION DATA

Stafford, Patricia.
    Dreaming and dreams / by Patricia Stafford; illustrated with photographs and with diagrams by the author.—1st ed.
       p.   cm.
    Includes bibliographical references and index.
    Summary: Discusses dreams, remembering them, controlling them, why we dream, and dream themes and meanings.
    ISBN 0-689-31658-5
    1. Dreams—Juvenile literature. [1. Dreams.] I. Title.
BF1091.S66   1992
    154.6'3—dc20   91-22898

To my dear husband,
Roy Mann,
the man of my dreams

ACKNOWLEDGMENTS

I would like to express my appreciation to all those who assisted me in research and supplied pictures for this book: Dr. Robert Van de Castle, Blueridge Hospital, Charlottesville, Virginia; Dr. David Faulkes, Emory University, Atlanta, Georgia; Jean Shrimmer, Art Institute of Southern California, Laguna Beach, California; Bret Burgess, photographer, San Clemente, California.

I would also like to thank the teachers who cooperated and the many children who sent me their dreams, particularly those I used in this book.
Billy Mitchell School, Lawndale, California:
- Jannette Vasquez
- Laurie Guerich
- John Gaynor
- Gabriel Gomez

Madison School, Redondo Beach, California:
- Diana Rozendael

Golden View School, Huntington Beach, California:
- Brooke Guest
- Julie Friedlander
- Chris Schwab

Los Cerritos School, Long Beach, California:
- Jeffrey Sorenson
- Justin Lazzara

CONTENTS

1	OUR SLEEPING BRAINS	1
2	WHO DREAMS?	4
3	ANIMAL DREAMS	8
4	WHY DREAM?	12
5	YOUR DREAMY BRAIN	15
6	SLEEP STAGES	18
7	THROUGH THE YEARS	21
8	DREAM THEMES	27
9	REMEMBERING DREAMS	33
10	CONTROLLING YOUR DREAMS	36
11	MEANING OF DREAMS	41
	GLOSSARY	*47*
	BIBLIOGRAPHY	*49*
	INDEX	*51*

CHAPTER 1

OUR SLEEPING BRAINS

A few faint murmurs and sighs could be heard from the quiet, dimly lit room—a room lined with a row of infant cribs. In each was a sleeping baby. Across the room, several strange-looking electrical machines lined the wall.

Two scientists stood viewing the sleeping infants in this laboratory. "The electrodes are all attached, Doctor. Now all we need are the results from these EEGs in the morning." The doctor's assistant was referring to the brain-wave machines called electroencephalographs—EEGs for short.

The row of babies slept peacefully, cuddled in their warm blankets. Cool, small rubber cups (electrodes) from the EEGs were fastened to their heads. The infants couldn't feel them, but these devices were carrying signals through wires to a series

DREAMING AND DREAMS

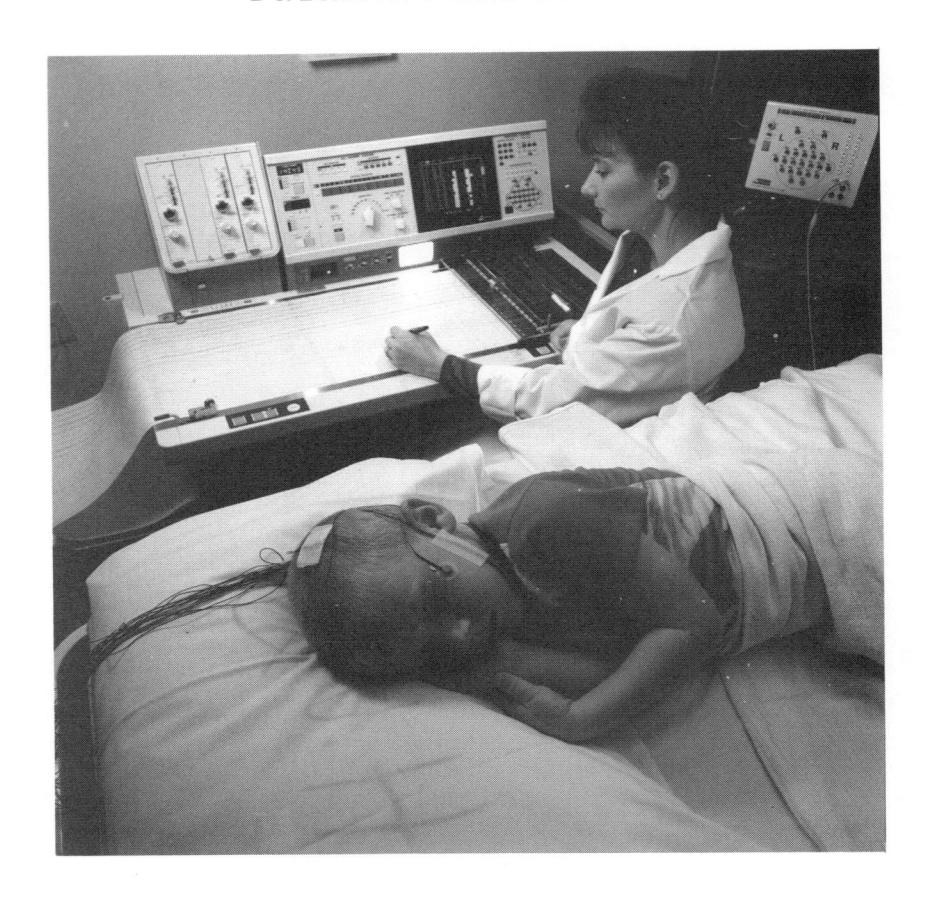

A dream lab assistant watches over a young sleeper.

of ink pens. The pens were zigzagging on rolls of moving paper. They were recording all the changes in the babies' brain activity and sleep patterns.

After making sure everything was in order, the doctor left for home. His assistant stayed to watch over the tiny sleepers.

The next morning, when the doctor returned, there were thousands of feet of paper on the floor. There had been so much brain activity during the night that these papers could have been stretched more than three times the length of a football field.

Eagerly the scientists studied the chart paper. It was filled with squiggly lines like ocean waves. There were high waves when the sleeping babies' brains were active and low waves during their quiet sleep periods. But the babies' brains were amazingly active. Before these studies, scientists had thought that people's brains quieted down and were very inactive during sleep.

Dr. Nathaniel Kleitman, with his assistant, Eugene Aserinsky, were conducting a study of sleeping babies at the University of Chicago in the 1930s. This was the first of what have been called "sleep for science" experiments, For the first time, people, through scientific experiments, were attempting to unfold the mysteries of our sleep world—our dreamworld.

CHAPTER 2

WHO DREAMS?

Eugene Aserinsky had become particularly interested in eye movements. He noticed that as people of any age sleep, their eyes go through periods of twitching and moving. To find out what it means, he decided to conduct an experiment.

Eight-year-old Armond Aserinsky was asleep on a cot in a small, strange room in the University of Chicago physiology department. He looked weird, with little black electrodes taped near his eyes. Wires from the electrodes reached to a nearby table on which rested an antique brain-wave machine that had been found in the basement.

Aserinsky was using his son for this experiment. He wanted to record the eye movements of a person during sleep stages.

Who Dreams?

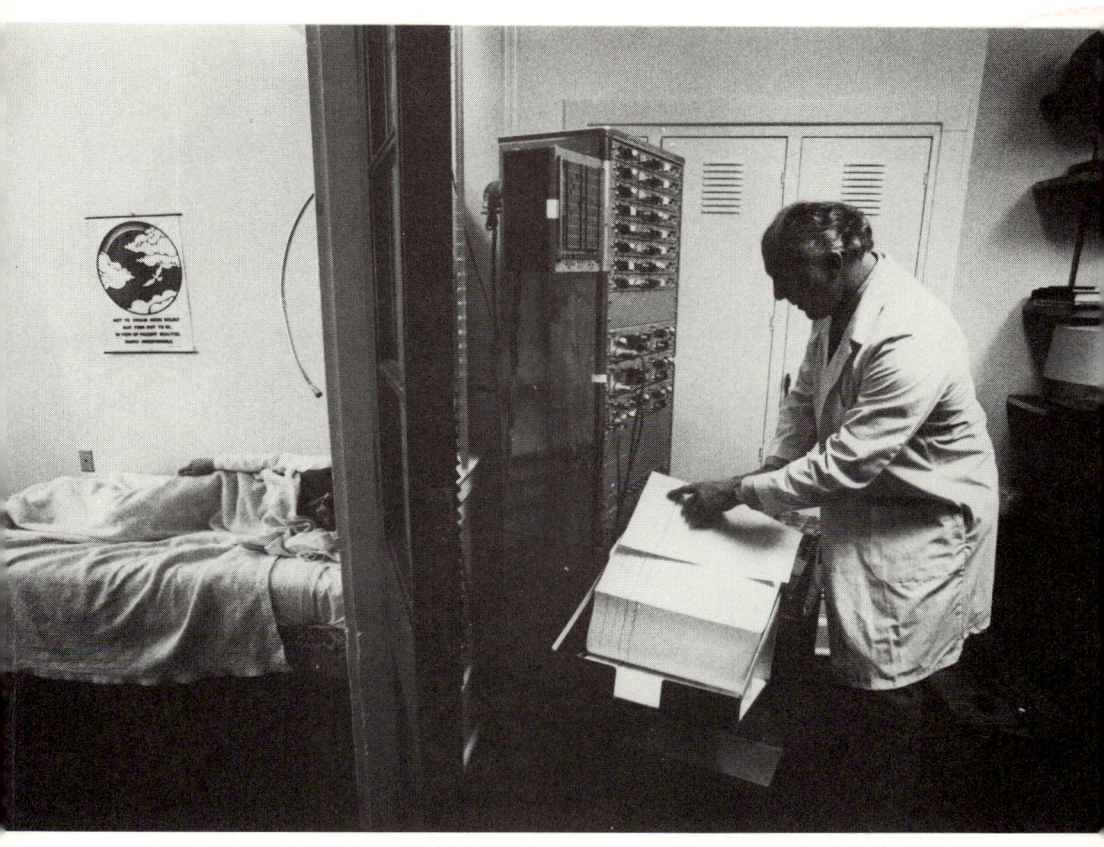

Dr. Robert Van de Castle checks EEG reading in his dream laboratory. (ROBERT VAN DE CASTLE, ASSOCIATION FOR THE STUDY OF DREAMS)

Data on eye movements had been gathered before, but nobody had stayed up all night watching and recording every one.

As Armond slept, his eyes moved up and down and side to side, as if he were awake. Sometime his eyes moved quite rapidly. Suddenly the movements disappeared for a time; then they reappeared. The EEG showed that there was a set pattern to the eye-movement periods that occurred on and off regularly throughout the night.

5

DREAMING AND DREAMS

With this experiment Aserinsky discovered a new stage of sleep that he called rapid eye movement, or REM for short. This term, REM, is in use today.

But Aserinsky wasn't finished. He was still very curious about dreams. He wondered if the REM sleep period was the time we dream and if Armond's eyes were moving because he was looking at something.

Now Aserinsky and Kleitman began sleep research in earnest. Many others became interested also. There are now dream research centers throughout the world. Adults and college students are paid a small fee to spend their nights in dream research laboratories.

Research has proved that all people do dream. Most dream four or five dreams a night during REM sleep. This was discovered by waking people during each REM stage. In all but a very few cases, the awakened people could relate what they were dreaming. More recent studies show that dreaming sometimes occurs during non-REM periods, but it is easier to recall those of REM sleep. Dream researcher Dr. David Faulkes believes that the thoughts of non-REM sleep later become a part of our REM dreams.

One question researchers asked was: If rapid eye movement happens because we are watching something like a dream movie, do blind people dream? Ian Oswald conducted experiments in Edinburgh, Scotland. While volunteers who had been blind since birth slept, the EEG showed the same brain waves as sighted people, but their eyes didn't move. They reported dreams of touch, smells, and sounds. Those who had lost their sight later in life continued to dream in pictures and did have eye movement.

All people dream: mothers, fathers, grandparents, teachers, TV stars, doctors, fighter pilots, and even the president of the

Who Dreams?

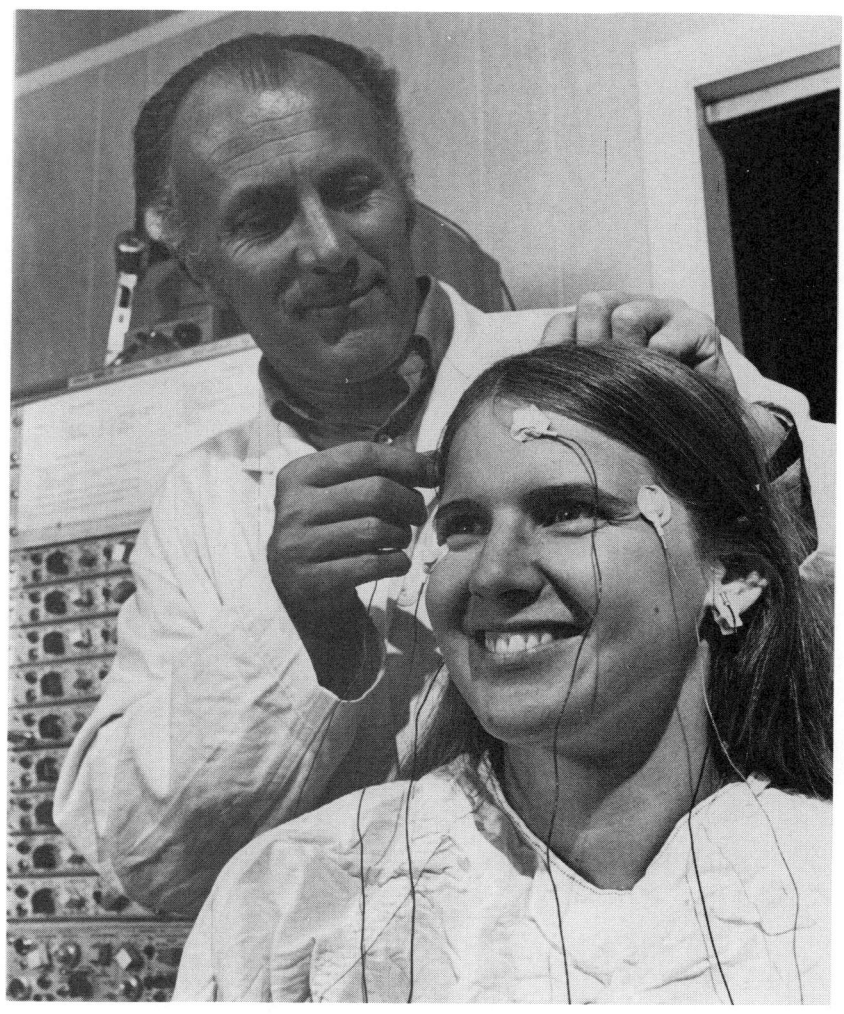

*Dr. Van de Castle attaches electrodes
from EEG machine to head of college student.*
(ROBERT VAN DE CASTLE, ASSOCIATION FOR THE STUDY OF DREAMS)

United States. Some remember their dreams very clearly, particularly the last one just before they awaken. Others think they don't dream. But they do. They just don't remember their dreams.

CHAPTER 3

—

ANIMAL DREAMS

"Look at Tiger," said Brian as he watched his cat. "He's asleep, but his tail's twitching. Once in a while he jerks and moans. He must be dreaming. Do animals dream?"

Brian's question is one that is often asked. Most of us imagine that our pets are dreaming when they move or groan in their sleep, but we aren't sure.

Researchers have studied all kinds of sleeping animals. Although we can't ask animals to tell us their dreams, there's strong evidence that at least most mammals dream. A mammal is a warm-blooded animal that has a spine and usually has hair; the female gives milk to its young. Mammals include humans, dogs, cats, horses, whales, dolphins, and many others.

Human brains and the brians of other mammals aren't

Human

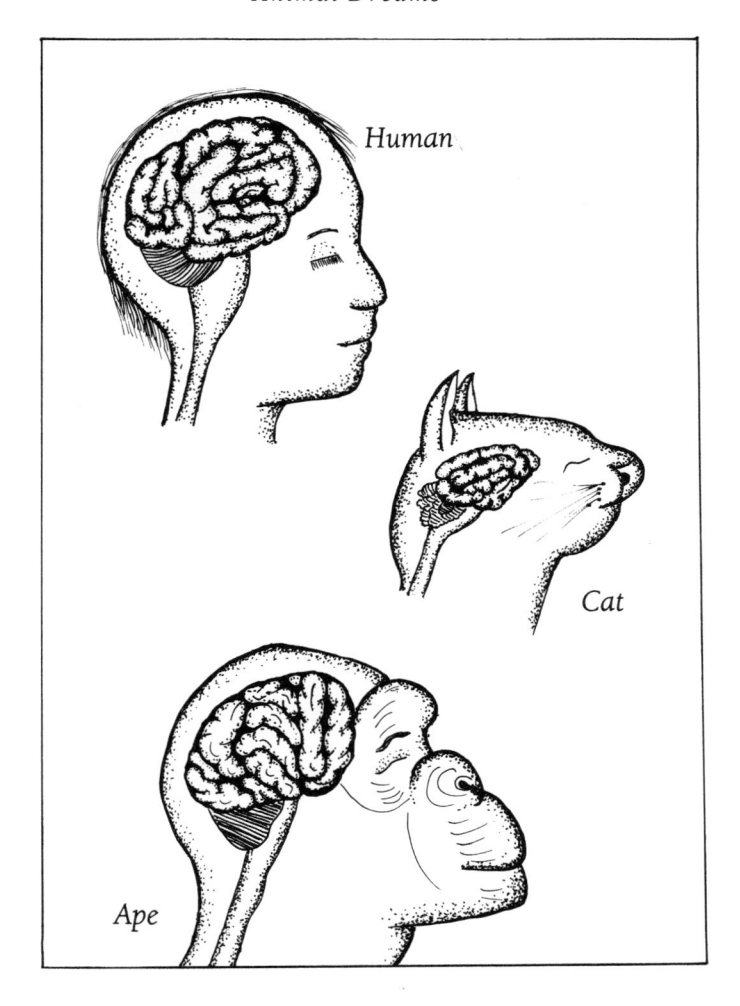

Cat

Ape

exactly alike but are very similar. EEG brain tests show that most mammals go through periods of REM sleep.

One day some scientists put several monkeys in cages where the monkeys could see a picture screen. The scientists trained the monkeys to push a lever whenever a picture came on the screen. Sometime later the scientists noticed that occasionally the monkeys pressed the levers while they were sleeping. No pictures were on the screen and the monkeys' eyes were closed tight. Thus it was believed that the monkeys were pushing the levers when they saw pictures in their dreams.

There are differences in sleep patterns among animals. Nocturnal animals are active at night and sleep in the daytime. Animals such as horses and cows can sleep standing up but only dream while lying down.

Then there are two mammals that don't seem to dream at all. In Australia there is a small, unlovely creature called an echidna. It has a long snout, spiny skin, and a sticky tongue with which it laps up ants and termites. This strange mammal doesn't show the type of brain waves that are the telltale sign of dreaming. Scientists discovered that one area of the echidna's

Echidna

Bottle-nosed Dolphin

brain is unusually large. They are trying to discover if this has a meaning for its dreamless state.

The other nondreamer is the dolphin. These mammals don't show any sign of REM sleep. Lev Mukhametov, a Soviet scientist, discovered that bottle-nosed dolphins sleep with only half their brains at a time. The two sides take turns: one half awake while the other sleeps. Scientists wonder if this is the reason dolphins don't dream.

What do animals dream about? We can guess, but we probably will never know unless we can teach them to communicate with us. But scientists are pretty sure that when your pet appears to be dreaming, it probably is.

CHAPTER 4

WHY DREAM?

Why do we dream? This remains something of a mystery, but it's believed that both sleep and dreams are necessary for a healthy life.

One night in 1959 Dr. William Dement and Dr. Charles Fisher were investigating the problem of what would happen if a person were deprived of dreams. As students slept in a dream laboratory, the researchers closely watched the EEG. Each time it showed that a student was beginning a REM period (which meant he was beginning to dream), they awoke him immediately. They did this all night, again and again. At first the students, who were used to being awakened near the end of a dream, not at the beginning, were puzzled.

For many nights the scientists continued to awaken the sleepers at the beginning of each REM period. This prevented

Why Dream?

*The more children dream, the better they remember
a bedtime story.*

them from having any dreams. All who were deprived of dreams were upset and grouchy during the following day. After several nights deprived of dreams, the students were very nervous and in bad moods all day. They had difficulty studying or concentrating. Some scientists think that a person deprived of REM sleep long enough would go insane.

The REM sleep of newborn babies is twice as long as that of five-year-olds. REM sleep, scientists believe, helps the brain develop. Studies show that the more children dream, the better they remember a bedtime story. People have their most creative ideas just before sleep and think best in the period soon after awakening.

Dreams could be safety valves to relieve our worries, tensions, and unfulfilled wishes. They may have a way of renewing our energy and giving balance to our lives. It seems as though our dreams are good for us.

CHAPTER 5

YOUR DREAMY BRAIN

Researchers have discovered some answers to questions about the brain and dreaming, although many others remain a mystery. The largest part of your brain, the cerebrum, controls what you learn and remember by processing and storing information like a computer. The cerebrum has two halves called the right and left hemispheres. These two sides are connected by millons of nerves called the corpus callosum.

The brain is a pinkish gray color and wrinkled. It feels like jelly. If a brain were laid on a table, it would spread out to cover an area larger than your pillowcase. That may all sound revolting to you, but the brain is the most wonderful body part we have. Without a brain we couldn't walk, talk, eat, sleep, breathe, or dream.

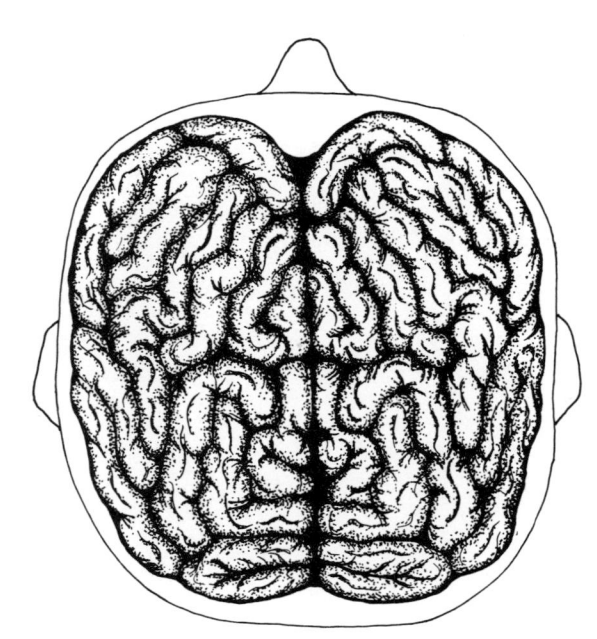

DREAMING AND DREAMS

Left	**Right**
Logic	Visualization
Order	Wholeness
Reasoning	Creativity
Analysis	Artistry
Sequencing	Problem-solving
Numbering	Bright ideas
Categorizing	Imagination
Mathematics	Intuition
Verbalization	Feeling
Reading	Expression
Writing	Music
Talking	Dreaming

Researchers have determined that each side of the brain, the right and left hemispheres, performs different tasks. In most people the left side is the logical one and the right is creative. For the most part, the left controls all verbal tasks such as reading, writing, and talking. It is reasonable, logical—it makes sense.

The right side is very different. It's artistic and creative. It's visual and sees things as a whole rather than in parts. It's not one bit logical but is good at solving problems in a creative way. It gets bright ideas. This right side is full of imagination.

Your Dreamy Brain

Can you now tell, by reading about the tasks of the two sides of the brain, which side is mostly working for you while you're dreaming? Think about your dreams. Are they logical? Do they always make sense? Or are they often unreal, filled with imaginary animals, people, and places? Do they sometimes lead you through a land of fantasy and adventure, at times pleasant and other times frightening? If you answered yes to most of these questions, it seems as though dreaming, for the most part, is a right-brain function.

When you sleep, your left brain goes to sleep also and mostly seems to turn itself off. The mysterious right brain takes over to give you the images and feelings of your dreams. While dreaming, you are in a subconscious state, not aware of the real world.

CHAPTER 6

SLEEP STAGES

Tracy is propped on a soft pillow in her warm, cozy bed. She has just finished reading her favorite story. She yawns and snuggles farther down under the covers. She's relaxed and very sleepy, half awake and half asleep, but not yet fast asleep.

Tracy is in what scientists call an alpha state. This is the time when people often think great thoughts and get clever ideas. The creative right brain works best in the alpha state.

After a few minutes Tracy sighs, relaxes her muscles, and takes a deep breath. With a floating feeling, she drifts off to sleep. She is now in the first of the four stages of sleep everyone goes through each night.

Each night you too drift into stage one of sleep. This is the beginning of an unusual journey along unknown roads

Sleep Stages

with no clue to what lies ahead. You are on your way to your dreams where you may encounter wonderful animals, people, and places. But to get there you must go through several stages of sleep.

Stage one is a light sleep with slow heartbeat, even breathing, and relaxed muscles. You can easily be awakened. Then you go into stage two, a deeper stage of light sleep, when the EEG shows sharp spindles. This is followed by stage three, known as "quiet sleep." The EEG now shows great peaks and valleys. The heartbeat is slower and blood pressure and body temperature drop. This is called "sound sleep." Finally you are in the very deep sleep of stage four. It is very difficult to be awakened in this stage. This is the time of sleepwalking or talking in your sleep. In all these stages you have had no dreams.

Now things change. You begin to travel back up through stages three and two to reach, at last, stage one. But this stage one is different from the one at the beginning of your sleep. One difference is that now your breathing rate and heartbeat are rapid. You are completely limp; you can't lift your arms and legs. But the biggest difference is in your eye movements. Your eyes were still. Now they are moving rapidly: up and down, back and forth. You're now in the REM period of sleep. You are dreaming. You may be having all kinds of visions, fantasies, or adventures. If someone woke you now, you could surely tell him about your dreams.

During any night you will go up and down through these sleep stages five or more times. Nighttime experiences can be compared to a slow roller coaster ride. After the dream stage you go down through stages two, three, and four and back up to stage one. Each time you reach the peak of the roller coaster

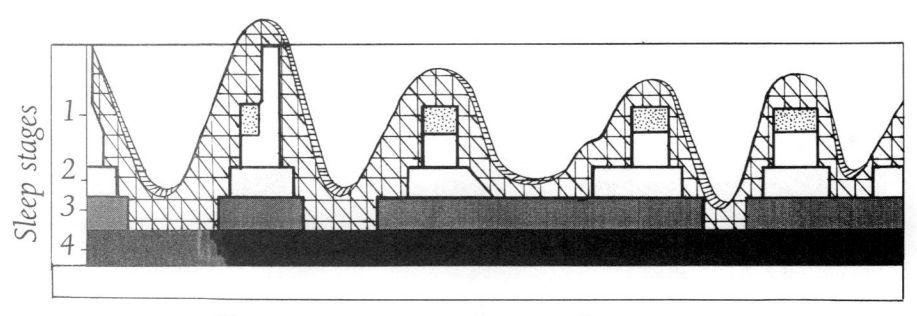

Sleep stages compared to a roller coaster REM

you have another dream. As you ride up and down, your dreams will last longer and you will spend less time in stages two, three, and four.

Although we have many dreams each night, most people don't remember them all. Dreams escape us very easily. You perhaps will remember only the last dream of the night. There are ways to help recall your dreams, though, and we will discuss them later.

Dreams usually occur about ninety minutes apart. Most people dream about 20 percent of their sleep time. The younger the people, however, the more time they spend at the roller coaster peaks—dreaming.

CHAPTER 7

THROUGH THE YEARS

No doubt even the earliest people puzzled about the meaning of their dreams. Throughout thousands of years of history they have inquired, studied, and come up with ideas about them.

Dream experiences, filled with monstrous forms and superhuman powers, caused primitive people to be aware of a mysterious, supernatural world. Perhaps this caused people to believe that we have a soul, a nonmaterial self that lives in our dreamworld.

Ancient Greek myths are believed to be symbolic dreams passed on through time. And what wondrous dreams they were.

DREAMING AND DREAMS

A pharoah's dream carved in stone (FRED MAROON)

Through the Years

Egyptian hieroglyphics record many dreams of kings. A pink stone between the paws of the Great Sphinx tells of a dream of a man who became pharaoh. In this dream a god spoke to him: "I will give to you the kingdom of Egypt and a long and prosperous reign." The god asked the man to notice the poor condition of the god's image, the Sphinx. It lay half-buried in the drifting desert sand. The god asked that it be saved from destruction.

People of the Old and New Testaments truly valued their dreams. They took them seriously, firmly believing that God would guide them in their dreams, or visions, as they were often called.

In the Old Testament numerous predictions are brought to God's children in dreams. Jacob dreamed of a ladder reaching to heaven. The Lord, standing above it, said, "I am the Lord, the God of Abraham, your father, and the God of Isaac. The land on which you lie I will give to you and to your descendants."

Dreams reported in the New Testament were the usual means by which God revealed his wishes. Joseph had four dreams that influenced the life of the child Jesus. In the first he was told to wed Mary. And in another, after Jesus was born, an angel appeared in a dream saying, "Arise, and take the young child and his mother, and flee into Egypt. Be thou there until I bring thee word; for Herod will seek the young child to destroy him."

The native peoples of Africa, Australia, and America have felt dreams are important too. Australian Aborigines believed that great beings appeared and guided them in their sleep. Native American boys went through a ritual at the age of puberty that included many days of fasting in a remote area

*Witches being hanged
(seventeenth-century print)*

until they experienced an inspirational dream that was to guide them for the course of their lives. This usually came in a dream of an animal that was to become their guardian.

During the first five centuries of the history of the Christian church, most church leaders believed dreams to be a direct contact with God. But things changed around the end of that period. Christians began treating the study of dreams as a form of superstition, magic, and witchcraft.

Saint Jerome was so influenced by this new idea of dreams that he mistranslated certain Hebrew and Greek words in the Bible. For example, "You shall not practice augury or witchcraft" was translated, "You shall not practice augury or observe dreams." (*Augury* means predicting the future.) Thus the practice of listening to dreams was now considered a form of evil and superstition. There are many stories of women who were put to death as witches because they were suspected of talking about dreams.

In the 1960s two clergymen did extensive research on dreams in the early church. They found that dreams and their meaning had not been considered evil but rather had been encouraged. Dream analysis had been a common spiritual practice to help make important life decisions.

Sigmund Freud, a famous doctor of the nineteenth century, developed a new theory of dream interpretation. It was based on dream symbols and called psychoanalysis. Freud believed that dreams have a hidden meaning—often a sexual meaning—that comes to us mainly in pictures or symbols. For instance, to him, a snake meant sexual conflict or evil, and fire meant danger. He asked his patients to tell him their dreams and he would try to discover the meaning. This sometimes helped patients overcome problems.

Later, Carl Jung, Freud's pupil, developed new theories. Both men based their dream analysis on symbols. However, Jung disagreed with Freud about the meaning of dream symbols. Freud believed that we can only dream of what we have experienced, while Jung maintained that each person has a soul and can dream of the future. Jung didn't believe that dream symbols represented sexual concerns or attitudes.

Today the study of dreams is no longer considered evil or superstitious. It's generally accepted that dreams reveal our wishes, fears, and daily contacts and that the meaning and control of dreams can be important to our lives.

DREAMING AND DREAMS

"Jacob's Ladder," by William Blake (BRITISH MUSEUM)

CHAPTER 8

DREAM THEMES

Did you ever dream that you were flying—not in a plane but under your own power? Many people do. Some enjoy flights over mountains and oceans. Others tell of floating above rooms in their homes. Flying is said to be the happiest dream theme people have. Flying gives a sense of freedom. Some say, "It gave me a lift."

Many schoolchildren have shared their dreams with me. Two of them were dreams of flying.

1

Once I had a dream. I dreamed I was flying all around the world. It was fun. I did not fall down. I landed at my house and after that I woke up! Oh, I did not have wings.

2

I had a dream that I woke up but was really sleeping. I felt happy like a dog that you just played with. I went to the stairs and jumped. I couldn't believe it. I was flying in my own house. I flew downstairs to get something to eat, but all I kept doing was hitting my head, so I decided to watch TV, but I couldn't reach the control, so I decided to go back to sleep and I woke up.

Frightening dreams of being chased and dreams of falling are quite common, but it seems we always awaken before we're captured or hit bottom. This boy did.

I was walking home from school with my friends when all of a sudden a witch jumped out from behind a bush. We were very scared. We started running. Too late—we had fallen in a big thornbush. Right before I was going to land on a sharp thorn, I woke up.

Most of us have frightening dreams at times. Some are just a little scary, but the most terrifying are nightmares. We usually awaken from a nightmare in a cold sweat and with a pounding heart. Nightmares can be terrifying experiences, but they are normal and can often help us understand our fears. Children often have nightmares after viewing scary movies or when something is bothering them. But as they grow older, nightmares occur less often. Two children shared these:

1

I was in a cave. There were demons running toward me. I turned into a jet. A demon was on my radar needle. He raised his knife. His body rapped on the glass. It was too late to pull up. I was about to crash and I woke up.

2
I was in a big room that had all different shapes and objects. Suddenly hands came out from the walls and from the floor. I was so scared I could hear my heartbeat pounding fast and loud. I came to a triangle-shaped room. It had fluorscent pink walls and pinhead people dressed in space outfits. I came to another room. I pushed against the wall and it opened and I woke up.

Children report frequent encounters with fierce animals, witches, ghosts, and, particularly, monsters. As they grow older these creatures are often replaced by real people they have come in contact with or figures from movies and TV. A boy shared this:

I was about to go to sleep when my bed turned into a monster and it started to chase me. I used my secret powers and turned into King Kong. Next I was Nintendo and the people came out from TV. I was about to get killed when I woke up.

Dreams are truly fantasies, for to fantasize is to escape from reality by creating unreal images. We often dream of people and places we know, but nothing in our dreams is truly happening. We also dream of unreal or superhuman people and places. Sometimes animals turn into people or people into animals. Many dreams are fun; our wishes come true, we go to exciting places and enjoy great adventures. Two boys shared these fantasies:

DREAMING AND DREAMS

I dreamed about I was a prenses and my boyfrend was a Prens.

One girl's wishful dream

1

I went to the air show and saw the Blue Angels and one of the men said, "You win a free ride." I was so excited that I said okay. After the ride he said, "You were so good and fly so well you win a free Blue Angel." So now I was a pilot.

2

My friend, Paul, and I were riding our bikes and ran into a Lamborghini and jumped off. Before you know it we were riding on top of a 747 and I used the tail for a ramp and jumped off. I landed on a mattress and bounced off. It ended I was on the news and doubled my allowance.

Dream Themes

Creative dreams can be very useful. Artists, musicians, and writers have had inspirations from creative dreams. Inventors have been inspired with ideas and scientists have received answers to problems in dreams.

The story of *Dr. Jekyll and Mr. Hyde* and their split personality came to Robert Louis Stevenson in a dream. Friedrich Kekule von Stradonitz, a German scientist, had been trying to solve a problem about the arrangement of carbon atoms in a benzene molecule. A dream of six snakes in a circle biting one another's tails gave him the answer that the molecules were arranged in a circle. Elias Howe had a problem working out his invention of the sewing machine; his solution came in a dream also. He dreamed of being captured by savages carrying spears that had holes in their tips. Upon awakening, he realized he should put the hole in the tip of the needle, not the middle.

The previous chapter told of spiritual or guidance dreams that were common long ago. In today's more materialistic, scientific world these kinds of dreams are less frequent. Some people, though, continue to report dreams that are wise, deep, and inspiring. The messenger may be a wise old man, a teacher, a priest, a rabbi, or Buddha.

Children who live in a home with a religious atmosphere are more apt to have dreams of God, angels, and heaven. Those who pray for answers to problems are often answered in dreams. It is possible for any of us to receive dream messages that solve problems, calm our fears, or inspire us to action.

Children often ask, "Do dreams come true?" The answer is generally no. Yet there have been cases of dreams that predict a future event when there's no way the dreamer could know it. Others report dreams of people, places, or events of long ago, when the dreamer had never had any information about these events or places. But don't expect to have these kinds of dreams. They are quite rare. Often people who think they've had this kind of dream don't realize that it's really a coincidence or that they've dreamed about information they'd received but forgotten.

CHAPTER 9

REMEMBERING DREAMS

Each of us dreams several dreams each night, but most people only remember their last dream before awakening.

We don't know for sure why some people recall dreams more easily than others. One theory is that those who don't remember really don't think their dreams are interesting or important. We are more apt to remember vivid dreams or nightmares because they make such a strong impression on us.

Some people don't recall their dreams because they jump out of bed quickly when they wake up and don't try to remember. Unless you have a nightmare, dream memory usually lasts only five or ten minutes. When we awaken naturally, we always awaken from a dream and can more easily recall it, but if an alarm or someone calling wakes us, we may not have been dreaming.

If you wish to recall dreams, wake up by yourself and keep your eyes closed until your mind brings back dream images. Pretend you're looking at a movie screen. Even try to see the color. We do dream in color, but color memory fades faster than the dream itself. Often you will recall one small thing, but if you keep thinking, more of the dream will come to you.

Try telling someone your dream as soon as you can. But better still, try writing your dreams. Keep a dream diary or draw pictures of your dreams. It can be interesting to read about them later to see if there's a common theme or something you dream of again and again. Often you can get ideas of thing that may be bothering you and solve problems you didn't know you had.

To record dreams you have during the night, just say to yourself, when you are in that drowsy, relaxed, almost-asleep period, "I will remember my dreams tonight. I will wake up after each dream."

Dr. J. Allan Hobson of Harvard University, probably the world's best-known dream psychologist, tells us that the phrase "I will remember my dreams," repeated nightly, is usually enough to make you recall them.

Dr. Ann Farady, a psychologist and dream researcher, goes a step further. In her book *The Dream Game* she states: "When you are completely relaxed, say something like this: 'Dreams, I'm ready for you. I promise that if you send me a message tonight, I'll do my best to remember it and write it down.' Repeat this request several times and try to fall off to sleep with it on your mind."

Telling yourself to wake up after each dream can make it happen. It may not the first time you try. You may need to

Remembering Dreams

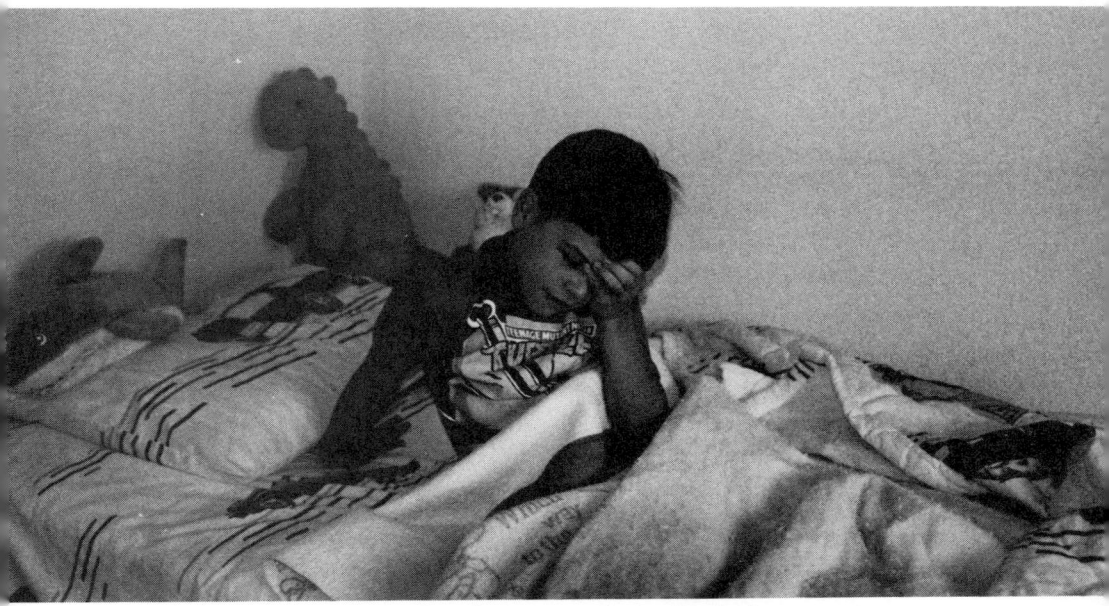

Brian keeps his eyes closed to try to bring back dream images.

do this several nights before you awaken after each dream throughout the night.

Some people tape-record or write their dreams. I decided to try. Every night for two weeks I told myself to wake up after each dream. Surprisingly, I did. By my bed was a tape recorder. Each time I awakened I told my dream aloud and was amazed to find six or seven dreams on the recorder each morning. Not only was I enjoying most dreams, but I had the added pleasure of listening to them the next day.

Your dreams can be pleasant and exciting adventures. If you think your dreams are important and you want to remember them, they will come to you with less effort and more often. Those who don't believe in dreams, or who think they are nonsense, won't remember them.

CHAPTER 10

CONTROLLING YOUR DREAMS

Far off in Southeast Asia lies the tropical land of Malaysia. In a remote rain forest live the Senoi, who are also known as "People of the Forest." The Senoi have become world famous for their ability to control dreams.

Six-year-old Palo, lying on a straw mat in a bamboo house built on stilts, has just awakened. His heart is pounding from the fright of a scary dream. He hopes he won't have a dream like this again. But Palo knows that soon he will get help from the family during the breakfast gathering where dreams are shared. Later, while the family sits on a circle of grass mats, Palo waits his turn as other children tell their dream stories.

Every morning from the time Senoi children can talk, they share their dreams with the family. In this way they learn how

Controlling Your Dreams

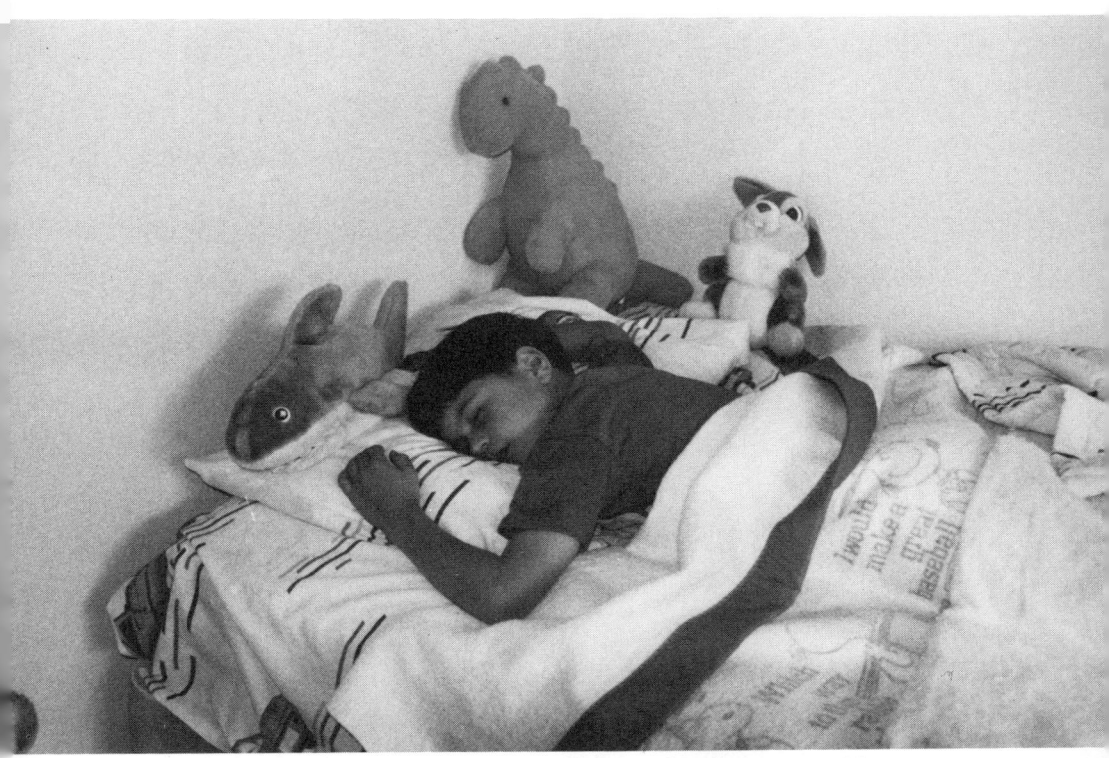

Brian, in a drowsy state, talking to his dream world

to control their dreams and solve everyday problems. Sometimes, when they have an unpleasant dream about a person they know, they are advised to give that person a gift. If they have a bad dream, they are taught how to make themselves have the same dream again and change it to a happy ending.

Senoi children learn three main things about their dreams: to face and control danger, to move toward pleasure in dreams (such as flying), and to always end dreams in a positive way. By practicing these things the Senoi enjoy a happy, peaceful way of life.

DREAMING AND DREAMS

If you wish to try controlling your dreams, you must think about dreaming before you go to sleep. Talk creatively to your dreamworld. Again that drowsy alpha state, just before you drift off, is the time you make suggestions to your dreamy brain. Tell it what you want to happen in your dreams.

If you have bad dreams of fierce animals, monsters, or evil creatures, talk to your dreamworld. Tell yourself that if an evil creature comes after you, you'll look it in the eye with a mean face and shout, "Don't you dare chase me. If you do, I'll come after you. I'll chase you off the face of the earth." If you prepare yourself to do this before you go to sleep, you can often make it happen. If you chase a creature away in your dream, you may never dream of it again.

Dr. Patricia Garfield, a dream psychologist, in her books *Creative Dreaming* and *Your Child's Dreams*, explains dream control at great length. She has personally visited with Senoi people in Malaysia and suggests their methods as well as others. Even Dr. Allan Hobson states, "I find myself in sympathy with Senoi-Malaysian people who discuss dreams every morning and control their dreams to their current concerns and actions."

Children who are very disturbed by frequent bad dreams are often helped by doctors in sleep laboratories. Dream researcher Ira Wile works with children to help them eliminate their dream terrors. He suggests several ways to do this. Some children are asked to choose something that they would prefer to dream about. Others are urged to tell themselves to sleep peacefully because their terror dreams are foolish. And still others are taken to see things they have been frightened of. For instance, a child who has terror dreams of fire engines is taken to a fire station to view the harmless engines.

Do you ever have dreams when you know you are dreaming? This is called lucid dreaming. You might just have one

Controlling Your Dreams

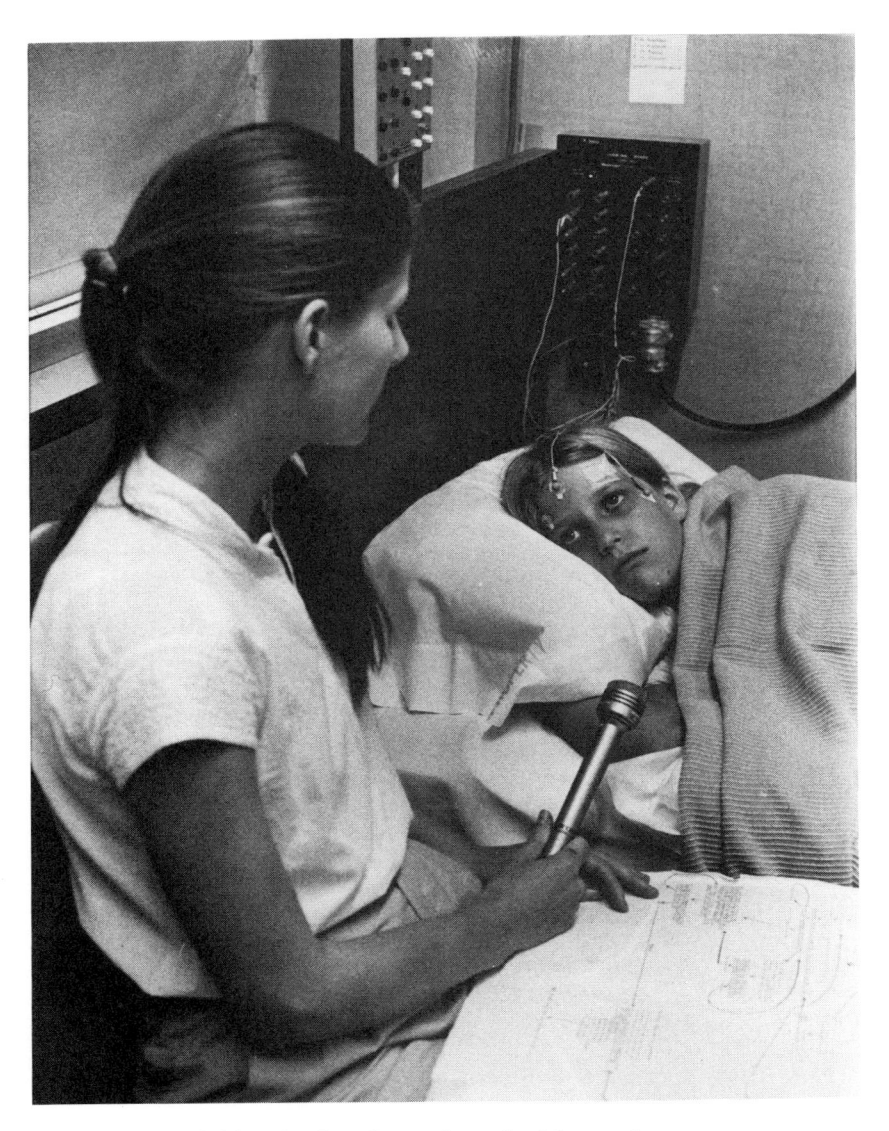

A child, who has been disturbed by nightmares, is helped by a doctor in a sleep laboratory.
(DAVID FAULKES, PH.D., EMORY UNIVERSITY)

thought, during the dream, that you are dreaming, or the whole dream can be a lucid one. Those who study dreams have discovered that lucid dreams are the easiest to control. Those who practice lucid dream control report that when they know they are dreaming, they can make themselves fly or have many other experiences that are enjoyable.

Many dream researchers today are engrossed in studies of lucid dreams. The first extensive study of lucid dreams and their control was done by Marquis Marie Jean Léon d'Hervey de Saint-Denys over one hundred years ago. He had a collection of the dreams of 1,946 nights that he had recorded since boyhood. He reported lucid dreams on an average of two out of every four nights.

Today extensive studies are taking place at Stanford University under the direction of Stephen LaBerge. In his laboratory work he has proved that it is possible not only for a dreamer to know that he is dreaming in a dream, but to take charge of that dream as well.

Some people can't get control of dreams as quickly as others, but it's helpful to try. Keep talking to yourself before you drift into dreamland. Like the Senoi, you might gradually change your dreamworld, eliminate fearful nights altogether, and truly enjoy nights of adventure.

In her book *Creative Dreaming*, Patricia Garfield sums it up this way: "Dreams in which you are overwhelmed by your dream images, chased, abused, ignored, or frustrated can leave you with a 'dream hangover,' clouding your waking activities. Dreams in which you successfully confront danger, have fascinating experiences, and discover creative products can leave you feeling covered with 'dream dust,' confident, happy, and full of zest for waking life."

CHAPTER 11

MEANING OF DREAMS

Some dreams are easy to interpret. Others can be very puzzling. Dreamers might find help or assurance in talking them over with family or friends, but no one—not parents, a doctor, or a best friend—can understand other people's dreams better than the dreamers themselves. Dreams contain one person's thoughts and ideas only, and no one else can really analyze them.

Dreams can be filled with symbols: people or things that represent something else. There are many books on store racks listing the meaning of dreams symbols, but no list of symbols can be right for everyone everywhere. Each person is unique, different from any other person. Symbols that often appear in dreams can mean different things to different people.

DREAMING AND DREAMS

Warmth and comfort

Fire and sparks

"Help! Fire!"—disaster

Sportsmanship

Liberty—freedom

Meaning of Dreams

To dream of a giant might mean a big bad man to some people. To others it could represent just a large person. Snakes can be interesting to some, yet the meaning usually given to the snake symbol is that it is evil. A monster is terrifying to most, but there might be others to whom it is no worse than the Cookie Monster. Kings and queens are usually considered authority figures representing parents or teachers, but in some dreams they might mean just the pictures on playing cards. A dog can mean friendship and safety to some but fear to others.

A good example of a symbol that can represent many different things, depending on the person, is fire. It can mean warmth and comfort on a chilly day or a feeling of energy as the sparks fly. Or it could represent disaster or tragedy to those who have experienced a damaging fire. Then too, fire could mean sportsmanship for the torch carried at the Olympic Games or freedom for the torch that is held high by the Statue of Liberty.

Gayle Delaney, Ph.D., a noted dream psychologist, has devoted her practice to teaching people to teach themselves and others how to understand dreams. In her book *Living Your Dreams* she tells about dream interviewing. "In dream interviewing, you ask the producer of the dream to tell you what it means. Since you produce your own dreams, you know what each symbol represents. Dream interpretation is a matter of learning to ask yourself the right questions that will jog your memory and remind you of what a part of you knew all along."

The Greek philosopher Aristotle, when discussing this subject, said, "Interpretation is a tricky business. Anyone may interpret dreams that are vivid and plain, but dreams are like forms reflected in water . . . if the motion of the water is great, the reflection has no resemblance to the original."

DREAMING AND DREAMS

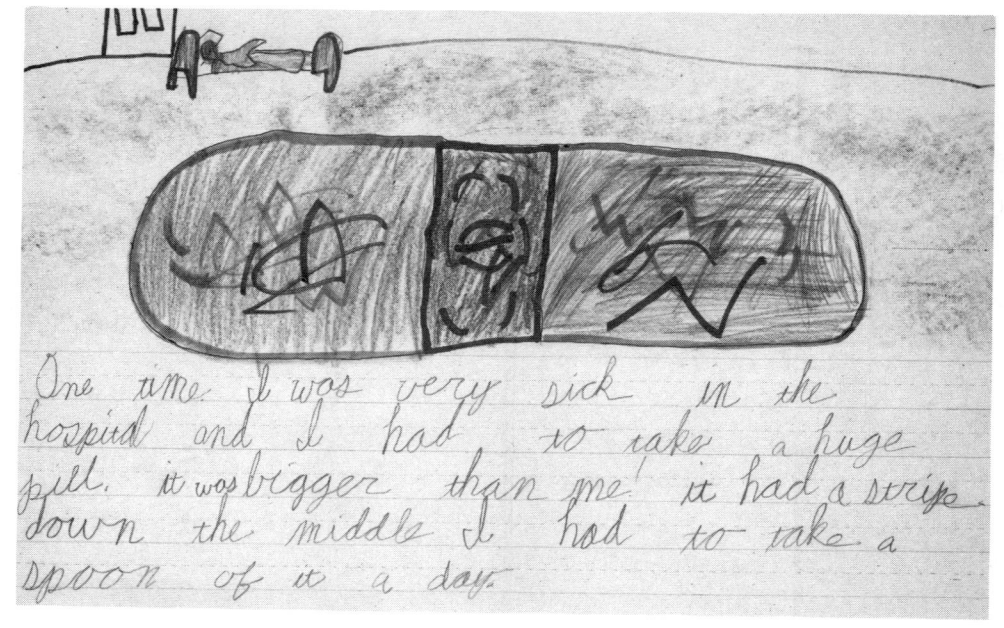

One time I was very sick in the hospital and I had to take a huge pill. it was bigger than me. it had a strip down the middle I had to take a spoon of it a day.

A child's fearful dream

Dreams may bring messages from the inner self: your subconscious mind. These messages can tell you about something that was perhaps bothering you during the day, though you might not have been aware of it. It's usually something that has been on your mind the last few days, but it can be something from long ago that you have been thinking of recently, whether you realized it or not. Dreams are sometimes a cry for help or an expression of an unfulfilled wish.

If you want to figure out a dream, first relax and let your brain remember the dream as a picture. Let your mind fill with a free flow of memories, ideas, and feelings. Then ask yourself some questions: What is the most logical meaning of this dream? Does it have anything to do with a problem I've had

Meaning of Dreams

lately or something else that has been on my mind? Does it relate in any way to that book I was reading, the movie or TV program I saw? Could my dream have been influenced by the wind blowing, the rainstorm, a telephone ringing, or any other outside sounds while I slept?

Be aware that you may have bad dreams about people in your life. You may dream of hurting them in some way or feeling happy if they are injured or killed. This doesn't mean you really wish them harm. The dream might be because you had had a recent argument or disagreement with that person, or the person may represent someone else entirely.

As you answer questions about your dream, you might now get some idea of the meaning. Don't try to be too literal or logical. We all know that dreams are anything but logical. They often seem to make no sense at all. In *The Dream Book*, Olga Litowinsky reminds us: "The mind is complicated, and its thoughts can't be put into a neat and tidy system, and so don't try to impose a system around your dreams where none exists."

Sometimes it is helpful to talk over your dreams with family or friends. One parent I know encourages her children to share their "fairy tales of the night" each morning around the breakfast table. But remember, don't accept any meaning for your dream that doesn't seem right to you.

Some dreams are good, some are bad, and some are horrible, but even the bad ones can be good for you. Dreaming about something bad may help you feel better about it and rid yourself of anxiety.

Dreaming can be great fun. We hope that this book has answered some of your questions about these journeys of the night and that you will forever experience and enjoy the magic joy of dreaming.

DREAMING AND DREAMS

GLOSSARY

ABORIGINES The original inhabitants of a country.
ALPHA STATE A relaxed state of a person just before sleep.
AUGURY A practice of foretelling the future by means of omens or signs.
CEREBRUM The part of the brain that controls voluntary movements and mental activity.
CHRISTIAN One who believes and follows the teachings of Jesus.
CORPUS CALLOSUM The part of the brain that separates the left hemisphere from the right hemisphere.
CREATIVE Being able to bring into being new thoughts and ideas.
ELECTRODE Electrical conductor through which electrons enter or leave a conduction medium.

ELECTROENCEPHALOGRAPH (EEG) An instrument that detects and records electrical activity in the brain.
EXPERIMENT An investigation to prove or test a theory or statement.
GREEK The language and people of Greece.
HEMISPHERES Two halves of an object whose shape is roughly that of a sphere (a ball, a globe, the brain, and so on).
HEBREW The language originally spoken by the ancient Jews. One of the official languages of Israel.
HIEROGLYPHICS Pictures or symbols representing objects or words. Usually the writing of ancient Egypt.
INSPIRATION A stimulation of the mind or imagination resulting in creative thought or action.
INTERPRETATION The act of making clear or understanding.
MATERIALISTIC Concern with material rather than spiritual things.
MISTRANSLATE To make an error in changing words from one language to another.
MYTHS Stories of unknown authorship that express a belief of certain people.
NEW TESTAMENT The part of the Christian Bible that recounts the life and teachings of Jesus Christ and his disciples.
OLD TESTAMENT Writings that make up the Jewish Bible and the first part of the Christian Bible.
PREDICT To announce or declare beforehand.
PHARAOH The title of the kings of ancient Egypt.
PROSPEROUS Having success, wealth, or good fortune.
PSYCHOANALYSIS A procedure used to explore the unconscious mind.
SPIRITUAL Relating to sacred matters.
SUBCONSCIOUS Not completely conscious.
SUPERNATURAL Relating to something beyond the natural world.
SYMBOL Something that stands for or represents something else.
THEORIES Ideas that explain a group of facts.
VERBAL Relating to or made up of words.

BIBLIOGRAPHY

Borbely Alexander. *The Secrets of Sleep.* New York: Basic, 1986.
Bro, Harmon H. *Edgar Cayce on Dreams.* New York: Warner, 1968.
Delaney, Gayle. *Living Your Dreams.* New York: Harper, 1988.
Evans, Christopher. *Landscapes of the Night.* New York: Viking, 1985.
Facklam, Margery, and Howard Facklam. *The Brain.* New York: Harcourt, 1982.
Faraday, Ann. *The Dream Game.* New York: Harper, 1976.
———. *Dream Power.* New York: Berkley, 1986.
Garfield, Patricia. *Creative Dreaming.* New York: Ballantine, 1974.
———. *Your Child's Dreams.* New York: Ballantine, 1984.
Gendlin, Eugene T. *Let Your Body Interpret Your Dreams.* Wilmette, Illinois: Chiron, 1986.

Hales, Dianne R. *The Complete Book of Sleep.* New York: Addison, 1981.

Hobson, J. Allan. *The Dreaming Brain.* New York: Basic, 1988.

Hudson, Liam. *Night Life.* New York: St. Martin's, 1985.

Hyde, Margaret. *Is the Cat Dreaming Your Dream?* New York: McGraw-Hill, 1980.

Kettelkamp, Larry. *Dreams.* New York: Morrow, 1968.

Lemaster, Leslie J. *Your Brain and Nervous System.* Chicago: Children's, 1984.

Lindsay, Rae. *Sleep and Dreams.* New York: Watts, 1978.

Litowinsky, Olga and Bebe Willoughby. *The Dream Book.* New York: Coward-McCann, 1978.

Mackenzie, Norman. *Dreams and Dreaming.* New York: Vanguard, 1965.

Mayle, Peter. *A Dreamer's Guide to Dreams, Nightmares, and Things That Go Bump in the Night.* New York: Crown, 1986.

McDonald, Phoebe. *Dreams.* Baton Rouge, Louisiana: Topaz, 1985.

Milios, Rita. *Sleeping and Dreaming.* Chicago: Children's, 1987.

Noone, Richard. *In Search of the Dream People.* New York: Morrow, 1972.

Silverstein, Alvin, and Virginia B. Silverstein. *The Mystery of Sleep.* New York: Little, 1987.

———. *Sleep and Dreams.* New York: Harper, 1974.

Stafford, Patricia. *Your Two Brains.* New York: Atheneum, 1986.

INDEX

Alpha state, 18, 28
Animals
  brains of, 8–9
  dreams of, 8–11
  nondreamers, 10–11
Aristotle, 43
Aserinsky, Armond, 4–6
Aserinsky, Eugene, 3–4, 6
Augury, 25

Bible. *See* Old and New Testament
Blind people
  and dreams, 6
Brain
  of animals, 8–9
  description, 15
  human, 8–9, 15–17
  tasks and functions of, 16–17
Brain activity, 1–3, 6, 10
  of babies, 1–3
Brain waves, 1–4, 6, 10

Cerebrum, 15
Chicago, University of, 3–4
Christian church
  and dreams, 24–25
Corpus callosum, 15

Delany, Gayle, 43
Dement, William, 12
Dolphin, 8, 11
Dream deprivation, 12–13
Dream interviewing, 43
Dreams
  advantages of having, 12–14, 23, 25, 27, 31, 35, 37, 40, 44–45
  blind people and, 6
  children's, 27–32
  Christian church and, 24–25
  color in, 34
  control of, 25, 36–40
  creativity, 14, 16, 18, 31, 40
  diary of, 34
  fantasy in, 17, 19, 29–30
  fire symbols in, 42–43
  flying in, 27–28, 37, 40
  frightening, 17, 28–29, 33, 36–38, 40, 45
  historical, 21–25
  inventions and, 31
  length of, 13
  lucid, 38, 40
  meaning of, 21–25
  monsters in, 29, 43
  number of, 6, 19–20, 30
  pleasant, 17, 29–30, 35, 37

Index

Dreams (cont.)
  predictions in, 23–25, 31–32
  problem-solving in, 31, 34, 44
  recall of, 6–7, 19–20, 33–35
  recording
    drawing, 34
    keeping diary of, 34
    tape-recording, 34–35
    writing, 34–35
  sexual meaning of, 25
  spiritual, 23–25, 31–32
  symbols in, 21, 25, 41, 43
  telling, 25, 36, 38, 41, 43
  themes of, 27–32

Echidna, 10
Egypt, 23
Electrodes, 1, 4
Electroencephalograph (EEG), 1, 4, 7, 9, 12, 19
Eye movement, 4–6, 19

Faraday, Ann, 34
Faulkes, David, 6
Fisher, Charles, 12
Freud, Sigmund, 25

Garfield, Patricia, 38, 40
Guidance dreams. *See* Dreams, spiritual

Hervey de Saint-Denys, Marquis Marie Jean Léon d', 40
Hobson, J. Allan, 34, 38
Howe, Elias, 31

Inspirational dreams. *See* Dreams, spiritual
Inventions
  and dreams, 31

Jacob's dream, 23

Jerome, Saint, 24
Joseph's dream, 23
Jung, Carl, 25

Kekule von Stradonitz, Friedrich, 31
Kleitman, Nathaniel, 3, 6

LaBerge, Stephen, 40
Litowinsky, Olga, 45

Magic, 24–25
Malaysia, 36, 38
Mammals, 8–11
Monkeys, 9–10
Mukhametov, Lev, 11

Nightmares. *See* Dreams, frightening

Old and New Testament, 23–24
Oswald, Ian, 6

Psychoanalysis, 25

Rapid eye movement (REM), 6, 9, 11, 12, 19
Roller coaster, 19–20

Senoi, 36–37, 40
Sleep
  non-REM, 6
  stages, 4, 18–20
Sleep patterns
  of babies, 2–3
  of animals, 10
Sleepwalking and -talking, 19
Southeast Asia, 36

Index

Sphinx, 22–23
Stanford University, 40
Stevenson, Robert Louis, 31
Subconscious, 17, 44
Superstition, 24–25

Van de Castle, Robert, 7

Wile, Ira, 38
Witches, 24–25, 28–29